THE
PRACTICAL
JOKER'S
HANDBOOK

THE
PRACTICAL JOKER'S HANDBOOK

Featuring mischievously funny ideas from
well-seasoned practical jokers around the world

COLLECTED BY TIM NYBERG,
CREATOR OF THE DUCT TAPE BOOKS

**Andrews McMeel
Publishing, LLC**

Kansas City

08 RR2 10 9 8 7 6 5

ISBN-13: 978-0-7407-4198-2
ISBN-10: 0-7407-4198-5

Library of Congress Control Number: 2003114748

CONTENTS

INTRODUCTION

Whether you're mischievous, seeking revenge for a joke played on you, or just plain like to be goofy, nothing satisfies quite like a well-executed practical joke. A longtime practitioner of practical jokes, I set up a Web site with the sole purpose of collecting practical jokes from people around the planet. In this handbook I have edited and categorized practical jokes that offer both classics and new creative wackiness.

Some of the more "dangerous" practical jokes have been omitted (although you might still find some on the Web site—www.practicaljokebook.com). In my mind, the purpose of the art of the practical joke is to entertain both the joker and the jokee (usually in the form of time-released humor). With that in mind, please administer your chosen jokes in the spirit of fun.

Remember that unless you are a sadist, inflicting physical pain isn't really all that much fun—or rewarding—and may actually result in an ugly lawsuit, fine, and/or imprisonment. So pick your target and your practical joke carefully. Then, have fun!

P.S. And remember when you're in the middle of that ugly lawsuit, you never heard of this book! (There, that will serve as my disclaimer.)

Note: *Attributions have been left out of this book. If you contributed a practical joke listed here, you know who you are—and thanks. Chances were quite good that someone else also contributed a joke similar to yours—thanks to them, too. If you know of a great practical joke that was left out of this book, please visit our Web site for submission instructions. The Web address is www.practicaljokebook.com.*

Some of these practical jokes (particularly the special section lists) have been gathered from mass-distributed e-mails that were lacking attribution. If you are one of the creators, sorry we didn't know who you were so appropriate credit could have been extended.

Publisher's Note: We present this collection in the spirit of fun but we caution you that jokes "and particularly these jokes" aren't for everyone. Physical or mental harm is not intended so be cautious and prank at your own risk.

THE
PRACTICAL
JOKER'S
HANDBOOK

HOMEGROWN HUMOR

HOMEGROWN HUMOR

The old adage says, "Most accidents happen within a mile of home (so to avoid accidents, move)." Permit me to coin a new adage: Most humor happens at home. Those who you know well are often the best candidates for practical jokes. Whether you live with your family, have been sentenced to live in a dorm for four (or more) years, or are struggling to survive a summer camp situation, you can have fun messin' around with your house/roommates.

Late-Breaking News

Get up early to get the newspaper. Replace the middle of today's paper with yesterday's paper. Watch in quiet amusement as people can't find the continuation of the cover story!

Fragrant Foul Fish Shtick!

Hide a piece of frozen fish in someone's room. Once the fish thaws, the room will start to smell. I did this once in a college dorm room. The room was inhabited by two guys. They lit candles and sprayed room freshener all week, each swearing it was the other guy's laundry.

Mower Mishap

Rig a friend's lawnmower with a plastic bag full of feathers or fur and hamburger meat. Secure the bag of stuff with duct tape securely to the bottom of the lawn mower above the blade. When your friend starts mowing, the vibrating will slowly shake the bag loose, and then "fur" and "guts" will fly everywhere! This one is especially good if your friend has a small dog or pet.

Sledgehammer

Make a mallet, handle, and head out of balsa wood. Paint the head black, and the handle dark brown, so it looks like a real, lethal sledgehammer. When company comes to visit, throw it at them when they walk in the door. The utter shock and expressions on their faces are priceless.

Do *Not* Open!

Put a DO NOT ENTER sign on your room door.
Secure a piece of cardboard into the upper door
frame (opposite the hinge side of the door) so
the cardboard extends four inches or so into the
room. Close the door and leave it slightly ajar so
the door is holding the cardboard. Set a plastic cup
(Big Gulp size) filled with water on the cardboard.
When the door is opened, despite your warning
to not enter, the intruder will get doused.

Invisible Door

Tape clear cling plastic wrap (or window insulating
film) across the doorway of a very dimly lit room
and wait for some unsuspecting victim to enter.

The Practical Joker's Handbook

Redecorating on a Budget

When given the opportunity to house-sit (water plants and bring in the mail) for some friends, I was given a key and, with it, a license to cause all sorts of mischief. When the couple came home from vacation to their two-level townhouse, they found all of the furnishings from one floor moved to the other and visa versa. After their initial confusion, they broke into laughter, then called me on the phone and read me the "riot act" (tongue in cheek).

Note: Helping them restore their furnishings to their original location is recommended.

Remote Remote Control

Unscrew a universal remote control. Use wire cutters to remove the little infrared transmitter. Hide the transmitter in one room aimed at the TV and solder enough wire to it to reach a safe hiding spot. Then, solder the other ends of the wires to the rest of the remote in the other room. Whenever somebody is watching something important (e.g., the Super Bowl) and a big play is happening, start flipping the channels.

Hot Teeth

Rub the insides and juice of a hot pepper (or add a few drops of habanero or Tabasco sauce) on your victim's toothbrush, and wait for the reaction when they brush their teeth!

Note: Don't rub your eyes after doing this, or the joke will be on you.

Roommate in Jeopardy

Live with a *Jeopardy!* addict? You know, the kind
that invites you to watch with them so they can
show off how smart they are? Secretly tape an
episode of *Jeopardy!* on a rare day when they've
missed the show. Tape a few minutes of the shows
before and after it as well. Then, memorize all the
answers. The next day, turn on the television and
start the tape playing prior to them entering the
room. You will amaze them at how much *you* know!

Selective Power Outage

Come home early from work and unscrew all
the lightbulbs in the house. Then leave and return
at normal time. By then your roommates will
be totally confounded—flipping breakers and/or
calling the landlord to figure out why only certain
circuits are out.

Bungled Bulbs

Rig a new pack of lightbulbs by putting little dots of gray duct tape over the base of the bulbs. This will prevent the circuit from being completed and the brand-new bulbs will not work.

Holy Buckets!

If another person is in the kitchen with you and about to leave, ask them if they could wait a minute and carry some water out to the backyard to fill the birdbath on their way out. Take a plastic container and go to the sink. Run the water in the sink while pretending to fill the container. Lift the container out of the sink, faking its weight. Walk toward the person and accidentally trip with the bucket aimed right at them. They'll flinch, you'll laugh, and they'll laugh too when they realize they didn't get wet. Option: Fill the bucket with confetti—but be ready to help clean up the mess.

Tacky Trotter

Lay a clear plastic carpet runner (with those little points on the bottom to hold it in place on carpets) upside down from someone's bedroom door to the bathroom. When they get up in the middle of the night to relieve themselves, they'll be in a world of pain.

Chia Carpet

If you know someone with that fake grass carpet on their porch or deck, secretly pour cress seeds onto a section of the carpeted area and water it. The seeds should germinate on the damp carpet and the person will eventually notice that their carpet is growing!

Krunching Kitty

Put a piece of uncooked elbow macaroni in your mouth, then hold a small dog or cat and *gently* turn its head left and right, while biting down on the macaroni. It makes a *very realistic* cracking neck sound.

Stringing 'Em On

When your roommate is out for the evening, get a huge ball of string or yarn and have some fun. Run the string all over their bedroom. Keep spinning the web until you can barely get out of the room. Turn off the lights and wait until they enter the room—tangling themselves in your web.

Giant Bladder

If you live in a house or apartment where the bathroom is embarrassingly close to the living or dining room (within earshot), fill a bucket with water and hide it under the sink or in the bathtub. Excuse yourself during a meal or conversation, go into the bathroom, and start emptying the bucket slowly into the toilet. Do a couple of appropriate breaks in the water flow (like you have finally finished) and then start the trickle flow again. When you come out of the bathroom zipping up your pants, your company will most likely be in tears on the floor.

Cream Face

While a friend is sleeping put whipped or shaving cream in both of their hands. Then tickle their face with a feather or light finger touch. They'll cream their own face.

Finger Dipping

A classic camp prank (which I have heard about for years but have yet to see actually work): Dip the finger of a sleeper into a cup of warm water. It's supposed to cause them to lose control of their bladder.

Busted Bedtime

Rig a camp bed by removing the slats under the mattress and replacing them with a few 1" x 2" pine boards, which will quickly break when laid upon.

Umbrella Shower

Fill a folded-up umbrella with confetti (dots of paper from a paper punch) or baby powder. When the umbrella is opened your victim will trade one type of shower for another.

Bedtime Boogie

Hide underneath someone's bed and wait until they start dozing off. Start pushing up on their mattress, first softly, then more vigorously.

Rude Awakening

When a person is sleeping, quietly walk up to them, aim a flashlight into their closed eyes and, as loud as you can yell, scream "*train!*"

Warning: If your victim has a heart condition, this may be the last time they ever wake up.

Fake ID

When your friend (or spouse) isn't looking, remove their photo ID and tape someone else's face over their photo. Works best with a celebrity's face.

Musical Carpeting

Take the small electronic music button out of a musical greeting card and hide it under your carpeting someplace where there is lots of foot traffic. Fix the activation switch so that it plays the music whenever it is stepped on. It will drive your family (and pets) nuts trying to figure out where the sound is coming from.

Cable Problems

When someone is watching television and leaves the room for a minute, sneak in and change the television to a channel that has static on it. When your prankee comes back they'll think the cable is on the fritz. Enjoy watching as they search for the problem.

COOKIN' UP A BATCH OF MISCHIEF

Here are some great recipes for cooking up a mess o' fun. Remember, you can have a lot of fun with food—even without poisoning your victim.

Gross Recipes

SLIME

The Nickelodeon television shows have a humor staple of slime. Nickelodeon usually uses eatable slime (yeah, like you want to eat it) based on nontoxic substances like water, food coloring, and powdered sugar; applesauce and food coloring; pancake mix, milk, and food coloring; or pureed Jell-O. There are a lot of goopy nonedible slime recipes available. Here are two of them:

Slime Recipe One:

Bring two cups of water to a boil, stir in 1/2 cup of cornstarch, and add food coloring to desired color. Cool at room temperature. (**Warning:** May stain furniture.)

Slime Recipe Two:

Mix one cup of water with one tablespoon of Borax (available in a grocer's laundry section). Stir until completely dissolved. Separately, mix a solution of 50 percent glue and 50 percent water. Take about one quarter cup of each water/Borax and water/glue solutions and put them in a sealable plastic bag with a few drops of food coloring. Knead the mixture in the sealed plastic bag until it turns to slime. After working with the slime, remember to wash your hands before eating anything. (Always a good idea anyway, right?)

FAKE FECES

Mark J., a movie prop maker, shares this recipe for fun:

For the movie *The Burbs,* we had to make some fake dog poo (because actors don't want to step in the real thing). We had a mixture of canned dog food, bean dip, and various other nasty-looking food items. After mixing the concoction, we loaded it into empty caulking tubes and squeezed it where needed. It looked so good, we went over to the nearest park, placed a perfectly shaped "dropping," and waited for the next dog walker to come by. To a dog it looks and tastes pretty good.

Note: Replace the dog food recipe with grandma's favorite fudge recipe and you can plant a few strategically placed droppings prior to your walk in the park. Bend over, pick up a piece, and nibble on it yourself. If you aren't into baking, packaged brownies look like dog nasty when you roll them up like snakes.

VOMIT

In a blender combine tomato soup, creamed corn, and a bit of bread. Blend slightly so the mixture remains lumpy. Pour on the location of your choice (remembering that this will stain carpeting), or load a bit into a sealable plastic bag. Turn your back on your audience as you expel the contents of the bag (apparently from your mouth) along with the appropriate loud retching sounds.

Snot Funny!

Hand sanitizer secretly squirted into your hand right before you "sneeze" works great. Try to get the little travel bottles of milky white sanitizer—it looks the best and the bottle can be easily slipped in and out of your pocket. After you "sneeze" into your hand, do something disgusting with the "snot" like rub it around and then smear it in your hair.

Kitchen Shower

Fill an unbreakable cup with water and set it in an upper kitchen cabinet. Attach a short length of thread to the cup and tape the other end inside the cabinet door. When the door is opened, your victim will get a shower.

Eggsplosion!

Blow up a small balloon to near capacity and put it in a serving bowl. Cover the balloon with scrambled eggs and place the dish on the table. Place a fork in the bowl as the serving utensil. The first person to dig into the bowl will pop the balloon and distribute the eggs all over the table.

Just Half a Glass, Please

Place cling film loosely over the rims of wine glasses. Carefully push the plastic film about an inch down into the glasses. Trim off the excess film. Tell your guests to help themselves to wine; they will mysteriously poor only the upper half of the glass. Wine glasses with a rippled glass finish in a dimly lit room are recommended for successfully pulling off this prank.

Messwich

Create a sandwich that will leave quite a mess
when it's bitten into. Insert a piece of plastic wrap
as one layer of the sandwich. The bite will not go
through the plastic layer, rather pull out the plastic
and much of the sandwich contents along with it.

Sugar (?) Cookies

Bring batches of sugar cookies to work a few
times so people get used to how wonderful your
cookies are. Then substitute salt for the sugar
when they have come to expect the real thing.
Indicate that you have changed the recipe slightly
(to cut down on your sugar intake), but you think
they taste just as good, if not better!

Bad Gatorade

During sporting events, drink (or dump out) your teammates' sport drinks and refill their bottles with regular water, salt, and a few drops of food coloring to match the sport drink.

Pesky Possum Potable Poopy Prank

This prank was once played on a possum that wouldn't stay out of the garbage, although it would probably work equally as well on dogs or humans. Inject the cream filling of a Twinkie with a laxative. By the way, the possum ate it and never came back for more.

Note: You can get a food syringe for injecting the laxative at a kitchen supply store.

Tollhouse or Outhouse Cookies?

Replace the chocolate chunks in a cookie mix with chunks of crumbled Ex-Lax. Enough said.

Oreo Madness

A lot of folks suggest replacing the Oreo filling with white toothpaste. However, due to the potentially harmful effect of eating toothpaste, I'd suggest replacing the filling with a paste mixture of baking soda and water. Works great and tastes awful!

Pet-Food Lover

Wash out a can of cat or dog food and replace it with tuna or liver sausage. Walk into a room full of people casually eating out of the can with a fork.

Doggy Chowin'

Get a little sample-sized box of dry dog food from your local pet shop. Replace the contents with Cracklin' Oat Bran (or some other cereal that resembles dry dog food). Snack away! It's more effective if you make no effort to call attention to what you are doing.

Bag Lunch

If you pack a daily lunch for someone, throw them a curve someday. Fill their lunch box/bag with junk and a sandwich that consists of a crust of bread folded over a ten-dollar bill and a note that reads, "Go out and have a nice lunch on me." (Make sure the sandwich is near the top and the bill is obvious or they might throw away their lunch money.)

Label Switching

Canned goods often have paper labels that can be easily removed by soaking them in water. Lay the labels out to dry and then reattach the labels to the wrong cans. Your victim will be totally confused upon opening the cans.

Doggy Don't

Carefully smear some creamy peanut butter on the bottom of your shoe. Keep your foot off the floor so you don't get it dirty. Cross your legs and wait for someone to notice that you have stepped in some dog poop and point it out to you. Reach down and get a sample with your finger, sniff it, then put it in your mouth. Say, "Yep, that tastes like dog poop all right!" This usually sends a few to the restroom.

Rabbit Turd Treats

Next time you visit a friend who owns a rabbit or go to a petting zoo, take a few Cocoa Puffs with you in your pocket. Discreetly reach into your pocket and hold Cocoa Puffs in your hand. Reach into the cage and pretend to grab a few rabbit droppings. Display them to your friends, then quickly pop them in your mouth, chew, and swallow. "Mmmmm!"

Dish Soap Overload

The next time you are at someone's house for a party, sneak a hefty amount of liquid dish soap into the bottom of their dishwasher. When they run the dishwasher at the end of the party there will be suds all over the kitchen.

Eat Dirt!

This one came to us from a mischievous pastor in Minneapolis, Minnesota. He hates boring board meetings (can you blame him?). To liven things up, before a weekly meeting he placed a flower pot in the middle of the conference room table. Earlier, he had replaced the top half of the potting soil with crushed-up Oreo cookies. During the meeting, he reached nonchalantly into the pot and started grabbing small portions of "dirt," which he proceeded to eat. He eventually removed his focus from the meeting and became obsessed with eating the "dirt." It was stuck to his teeth and smeared on his lips and cheeks. One by one the board members became aware of the situation and their initial shock changed to unified laughter. The meeting was anything but boring.

Hot Cheese Puffs

Break a cheese puff in half (one of the original fat, puffy ones). Use a paper clip or a toothpick to hollow out a little chamber in the puff. Fill the hollowed-out section of the puff with cayenne pepper. Reconnect the halves. (If you dampen both ends, they'll weld themselves together.) When your victim pops these in their mouth, they'll shortly be experiencing some serious heat!

Extralong Cheese Puffs

Using the above wet-and-weld method of connecting puffs, create the world's longest cheese puff. Bury this extra long puff in a bowl topped with regular-size puffs. When an unsuspecting puff popper grabs the rigged cheese puff, they'll be on the phone to Guinness World Records.

CHEAT-Os

Styrofoam packing peanuts, painted with orange food coloring, make for some interesting eating when used to refill the cheese puff bowl.

Red-Hot Caramels

Make your own blazin' hot caramels by melting down caramels, filling a candy mold half full, inserting a drop or two of habanero sauce (or other hot sauce) and filling the mold the rest of the way with caramel. Wrap the cooled caramels in waxed paper and set in the candy dish at your home or office.

Warning: Some people have allergic reactions to hot sauce. But if you have a coworker who is continually bragging about their ability to eat spicy hot foods, this gag is perfect.

Expires June 1, 1972

Get a page of little clear return address labels and print your own expiration dates (any date over twenty years ago). Then go around sticking them on things like medicine bottles, packaged foods, and milk.

Really Fresh Chicken

Get a fried chicken bucket, without the chicken. Purchase a live chicken (pick out a very docile hen) and put it in the bucket. Bring your "bucket of chicken" to a party. When the party host/victim goes for the chicken and removes the lid, they will be nose to beak with a *live chicken!*

Note: If you can't find a live chicken, stop by the grocery store and get a fresh whole chicken from the butcher.

Yoking Around

You can "blow" the contents from an eggshell by poking a small pinhole in each end and blowing on one of the ends. This results in an empty egg shell. Replace the empty egg in the egg tray. Funny enough by itself, but if you want to really mess with someone's head, patch one end with white glue, then use a syringe to fill the eggshell with pudding.

Flooding the Formica

Fill water glasses *full* and turn them upside down on the counter so they look like they're drying. When your victim puts them away, they'll get doused. (The flip-over maneuver is accomplished by holding a piece of stiff cardboard on top of the brim of the full glass, flipping it, and sliding out the cardboard.)

BATHROOM HUMOR

Nothing says "funny" like bathroom humor. No, I'm not talking about "blue" humor—I'm talking about humor that actually takes place in the bathroom. It is here that everyone is equal, blue collar or celebrity, pauper or president. There is no other place on earth that better removes pretense and brings us all to a common plain with our fellow humans than the bathroom. So, let's have some fun.

Untidy Bowl

I'm starting off with this one because it has been sent in more than any other prank. Place cling-film over the toilet bowl (under the lid). Be very careful there are no creases.

Can-Did Camera

Before a party, set up a video camera in the bathroom and take about fifteen minutes of just the empty bathroom (toilet in plain view). When it's time for the appropriate guest to relieve themselves, gather the rest of the guests and sit them down in front of the television with the video tape playing. When the guest leaves the bathroom and finds everyone sitting around laughing at the television showing the room that the guest was just occupying, horror and hilarity will ensue.

Switched Gender

Swap the signs on the women's and men's rooms.

Pop Pot

Place a snap ball fire cracker (the kind you throw down on the sidewalk) under the toilet seat, and gently lower the seat. Your victim will sit down with a bang!

Toilet Shower

On most household toilets there is a pipe sticking up in the tank. Clipped into the top of that pipe you will find a small water feed tube. Relocate that tube from the pipe to under the lid of the tank, pointing toward the bowl. Carefully replace the lid so it holds the water tube in place. When someone flushes the toilet they will get soaked!

Shower of a Different Color

When visiting a friend's house, take a bar of soap from their shower. Shave off a thin slice from the soap and make a little hole in the soap. Fill the hole with red, green, or blue food coloring. Cover the hole with the thin layer of soap (wetting the soap layer will cause it to stay in place). Place the bar hole-side down in the shower stall and wait for some colorful fun!

Condiment Commode

Take a ketchup, honey, or mustard packet. Fold it in half and place it under the pad of the toilet seat where it comes into contact with the stool. When your victim sits down on the seat, they'll receive a messy condiment surprise.

Note: A pin hole in the packet on the side facing into the toilet will help direct the mess.

Alien Pee

At a crowded party, or nightclub with a line to the bathroom, crack a glowstick and then snip the end, emptying the glowing contents into the toilet/urinal. Hilarity ensues when the people behind you are shocked and amazed at your glowing urine! If someone comments on it, tell them nonchalantly that you just toured the local nuclear power plant. Or pose the question, "Have you ever been probed by an alien?"

Toilet Snake Attack

Purchase a rubber snake and tie a short length of thread or fishing line around its head. Tape the other end of the thread to the lid of the toilet. When the lid is opened, the snake will "attack!"

Bugged Toilet Paper

Unroll the toilet paper a couple of times and place a fake insect on the roll. Rewind the paper over the bug and wait for someone to expose the bug. The best part is they won't be able to get too far when seated on the pot.

Busy Stalls Stall Business

This is perfect for a business that has only one restroom. Grab a pair of boots and pants for each toilet stall. Set them up in front of the toilets and lock the stall doors. Your fellow employees will pace the floor nervously and finally be forced to leave work to relieve themselves. (In the men's room place a cardboard sign with OUT OF ORDER written on it over each urinal.)

Nine-Foot-Tall Man

If you wear cowboy boots, it's a hoot to use the toilet stall in a public men's room to take a leak. Remove your boots, place them in front of the toilet as if you're still standing in them, and stand with stocking feet *on* the toilet to do your business. People are amazed to see what appears to be a nine-foot-tall man taking a leak, because they can see your boots down at the bottom of the stall and also the top half of your body. I've had people say, "Holy cow! How tall *are* you?"

Smokin' in the Can

Put dry ice chunks into a toilet for a bubbling, churning, smoking throne room.

Warning: A side effect of too much dry ice is a frozen toilet . . . which, I guess, can also be funny but potentially costly if the toilet bowl cracks.

Hot Cross Buns / Numb Bum

Smear a thin layer of Icy Hot, Ben-Gay, or a numbing gel on the toilet seat.

Sticky Buns

Clear Karo syrup on toilet seats provides a sticky mess that stops short of the oft-reported but not recommended superglue on the toilet seat.

Phantom Plumber

The Phantom Plumber, as he came to be known, would sneak into the men's room and loosen the nut on the top of the urinal. Nothing would happen until someone flushed it. Then water would spray from the top of the urinal and the man would get *soaked* from the waist up.

Chicken Soup Shower

Remove the shower head from your shower and put two or three chicken (or beef) bouillon cubes in the head. When the victim takes a hot shower they will end up smelling strangely like chicken (or beef)!

Note: There are variations to this including inserting jelly beans, instant coffee crystals, hard candies, etc., into the shower head.

There's Always Room For . . .

When house-sitting, the final night before the owner's return fill their bathtub with cold water and ice cubes, then mix in multiple packages of Jell-O. It should set up nicely. (Turning the air conditioner up may help speed the process and preserve the surprise.)

No-Lather Soap

Go into a friend's bathroom with some clear nail polish and paint their soap with it. Cover the whole bar and the soap will never lather up.

Lousy Aim

Next time you visit a public restroom, come armed with a water-filled sport bottle with a squirt top. Select a stall beside an already occupied one or adjacent to an occupied urinal. Unzip your fly and proceed to squirt the bottled water on the floor and/or shoe of the adjoining stall. Add some sound effects to make it more effective. ("Whoa! Oops, missed!")

Medicine Chest Capers

Here's a way to catch nosy guests. Remove everything from the bottom section of your medicine cabinet. Hold a piece of cardboard (like a dam) up to the bottom shelf of the cabinet, then load whatever you want inside, like marbles, Ping Pong balls, or golf balls. Close the door and slide the cardboard dam out. When the nosy guest opens the medicine cabinet, the booby trap will catch them.

Bathroom Water Issues

Go to one of those bathrooms that have sensor toilets and put a piece of black tape over the sensor so the toilet never flushes. Or put it over the sensor on the sink so the water always stays on.

Booby Trap Rigging

Tape one end of a "booby trap" firecracker (the ones with the strings coming out of each end) to the toilet bowl and the other to the lid. When the lid is lifted—*bang!*

Trailer

Take a six-foot piece of toilet paper and attach a piece of duct tape to one end (half of the tape on the toilet paper, half hanging free). Place the paper and the tape (sticky-side up) on the floor at the entrance of the bathroom. When an unsuspecting victim steps on the tape, they will drag the toilet paper on their shoe.

Water Mix-up

Turn off the water feeds below the sink. This is confusing enough, but if you have a wrench and don't mind a bit of work, switch the hot and cold water feeds. (Remember to turn the water back on.)

Sticky Soap

Fill a liquid soap dispenser with pancake syrup.

Bathroom Sink Shower

A small piece of duct tape secured over the faucet (leaving it loose in the front) provides a surprising spray all over your victim when they turn on the faucet.

PHONE PHUNNIES

PHONE PHUNNIES

From prank calls as a junior high schooler to coauthoring a book detailing how to have fun at the expense of telemarketers, using the telephone as a source of amusement has been a staple of my lifetime of pranking. Turns out, I'm not alone. In fact, there is even a television show called Crank Yankers *that's based on prank phone calls. Here are a few ways to have fun with thanks to Alexander Graham Bell.*

Freaky Phantom Phones

Nab a friend's answering machine and record a new message on the order of, "This is the FBI. All calls being made to this phone number are being traced and logged." Set the machine to answer on the first ring, and hide the answering machine where it is not easily found (you can usually plug an extension phone into the machine). If your friend doesn't have an answering machine, it's even funnier. Bring your own prerecorded machine and install it when they aren't looking.

Is Max There?

Phone somebody, and when they answer ask for Max. Repeat this four or five times (using different people each time heightens the effect). Finally ring and when the person answers say, "Hi, this is Max. Have there been any calls for me?"

Bogus Recall Notice

When a friend purchases a new car and is bragging about it a bit too much, call their phone and leave this message: "This is Mr. Frank, the customer service manager from _____ [dealer name]. There's been a recall on your [car model]. It is very dangerous to drive your car in its current condition. Please return your car to the dealer as soon as possible. No appointment will be necessary, just come in between 9 a.m. and 5 p.m. We're sorry about this inconvenience. I assure you the problem will be corrected at no cost to you. And please, if at all possible, try not to make any left turns when returning the car to our service department."

Dialing for XXX

Change your victim's speed-dial numbers to massage parlor and escort service numbers.

Who Called Who?

Got caller ID? Next time your phone rings and you recognize the caller's name or phone number, answer it saying, "Hello, may I speak to (use a wrong name)?" The caller will usually be more than slightly confused and tell you that you have the wrong number. Repeat this as many times as possible.

Black Ear Disease

Rub some black shoe polish on the earpiece of the victim's phone (assuming they have a black phone). When they answer the phone, they'll get an earful.

Hello? Hello?

On older model phones you can remove the microphone from the mouthpiece of the handset. Your victim will talk into the phone but nobody will hear them. Or remove the speaker from the earpiece for similarly frustrating results.

Unplugged

You can create a maddening moment for those with more than one phone in their house by unplugging an extension phone from the wall. When the phone rings, they will answer the extension phone with no results.

Carnival Planner

After regular business hours, look in the yellow
pages and call places that rent carnival rides,
clowns, petting zoos, jugglers, caricature artists, and
even Porta-johns. Leave messages that say, "Hi, my
name is [insert your victim's name]. I'm setting up
a neighborhood carnival in [insert month] and
wanted to arrange for your services. Please call me
at [victim's phone number] tomorrow between
[list an hour or two]. Thanks." Try to be there
when they get the return calls.

Fun with Telemarketers

Although these aren't necessarily practical jokes, there is a lot of fun to be had at the expense of those people who are relentless in their attempt to bother you during your dinner hour. These are some of my favorite selections from a book I coauthored in 1996, How to Get Rid of a Telemarketer *(no longer in print).*

Confuse the Caller

If you're sure a telemarketer looms on the other end of your ringing phone, answer by saying: "Hi, I'd like to place an order to go," and continue by reading your favorite Chinese restaurant take-out menu. If the telemarketer doesn't do so on his or her own, *hang up!*

Create a Technical Difficulty

Interrupt by ignoring the telemarketer and saying, "Hello? Hello?" Click the reset button twice quickly, without hanging up, and repeat "Hello? Hello?" Follow by saying, "Well, whoever it was, they must have hung up." Then *hang up!* If they call back, repeat. If they call back more than three times, tell them you were just kidding, compliment them on their persistence, and *hang up* immediately!

Reverse the Charges

Next time a telemarketer calls, don't let them get their first sentence out before asking them for their billing address. When they ask "Why?" tell them: "Well, I'd be happy to talk with you, but I'm a telemarketing effectiveness consultant and I charge for my evaluation of your performance. I need to know where to send the bill." Listen for the inevitable "click."

Give Them a "Fair" Chance

If you are in the kitchen at the time of a call, set the oven timer for five seconds and interrupt the caller, explaining that he or she has until the buzzer sounds to deliver the pitch. Then hold the mouthpiece of the phone near the timer, press start, and yell, "Go!" When the timer rings, *hang up!*

The House Fire

This routine works particularly well with telemarketers selling furnace, chimney, or ductwork cleaning. Once you have identified their service, break into tears and sob, "Is this some kind of a joke? My house burned down last night! We lost everything!" If they offer an apology, accept it graciously and hang up. If not, slam down the receiver. Either way you've left them with something to wonder about for a while.

900-FONE-FUN

Allow the telemarketer to begin the sales pitch. At the same time, start breathing heavily into the phone. When they pause to ask if you have any questions, breath a bit louder and say, "What are you wearing?" Your phone should be clear in a second. Works with same or mixed genders.

Product Criticism

If the phone solicitor is selling encyclopedias,* deflect the call by saying, "Is this some kind of sick joke? Who put you up to this? It's well known in these parts that our youngest lost her life because of your encyclopedias! Why, if that shelf would've held under the weight of volumes M–Z, she'd still be with us today! A pox on you and your policy of using heavy, glossy paper and thick, hardbound covers!" Hang up.

*Modify script and scenario to fit product.

The Practical Joker's Handbook

Veggiebabble

Based on the theory that you don't have to actually be psychotic to act crazy, this routine causes most telemarketers to question their career choice. When a telemarketer begins a pitch, arbitrarily begin inserting the names of vegetables as they try to speak. After the first or second "rutabaga" or "broccoli" they should respond by saying, "What?" Reply by naming another vegetable ("okra" and "Brussels sprouts" work particularly well). The salesperson will begin laughing uncomfortably and hang up. You win.

Pretend You're an Answering Machine

If you've already made the mistake of saying, "Hello," pause for a second and interrupt the telemarketer with, "Sorry, but I can't come to the phone right now. If you could leave your name, number, and a brief message after the tone, I'll get back to you." Pressing one of the keypad keys usually passes for the electronic tone of an answering machine (the number "9" key works exceptionally well), but a brief, sharp whistle really annoys phone salespeople. When you hear the telemarketer begin their message, *hang up!*

Express Jubilant Disbelief

Once the telemarketer indicates they have a "special offer" for you, interrupt with "For me? Really? Oh, this is great! After the bank foreclosed and I maxed out the credit cards, I thought I'd never get another chance! This is unbelievable! I don't need to be employed to order, do I?" When you hear the awkward pause on the other end of the line, *hang up!*

The Old Codger / Old Crone

If the caller asks, "Is this the man [or woman] of the house?" tell them, "Just a minute, please," and pretend to hand the phone to "Dad" or "Grandpa" (or "Mom" or "Grandma") as the case may be. Then use your best "old codger" (or "old crone") voice and bombard the caller by repeating "Huh?" and "Speak up!" If they persist, go into a pointless, meandering, story that begins: "Why, back in my day we didn't . . ." Add drool-laden "slurp" noises for effect. The phone salesperson will soon give up.

Vacuum Sales

Is the telemarketer offering a "free" one-room carpet cleaning? Excellent! Don't pass this one up! Simply tell them to "Come right over! Right now! Because, believe it or not—what timing! This is great! You see, I'm fleeing—er, moving out of state—very, very soon. Everything is set to go, but this house is a rental and I'll never get the deposit back if I don't get this carpet cleaned. How soon could you guys get here? It will get blood stains out, won't it? How about identifiable fibers, like hair or that DNA stuff? You know, like in the O.J. trial? Say, you don't think he really did it, do you? You want to know my theory?" Again, run with this one as long as you can.

Hello, Sports Fans!

As soon as you identify a caller as a telemarketer, change the topic to sports: "Did you see the game last night?" Once you get started, keep going as long as you can and try to engage the telemarketer in a debate about coaching changes, quarterback controversies, pitching performances, etc., that involve his or her favorite team (say, for instance, the Green Bay Packers). If the caller works the sales pitch back into the conversation, say, "I'm sorry, I'd never buy anything from a Packers fan. Cheesehead." And hang up.

My Dog Ate the Phone Cord

Let the caller get about two sentences into the pitch while you establish the presence of a dog by employing your best fake muffled bark. Next, act distracted and apologize as you turn to yell at the fictitious pooch: (muffled bark) "No, King! Don't chew on that! Bad dog!" Add more muffled barking, then yell to someone in the background: "Crimony, honey, would you get the dog outta here? He's chewing on the phone cord agai–" At this point, hang up the phone or pull the outlet cord from the wall.

Your Cheatin' Heart

The perfect encounter for when you receive a call from a telemarketer of the other sex. As soon as the phone salesperson says "Hello, I'm with—" cut them off quickly with a semi-whispered "Look, I thought I told you never to call me here." When they say, "Excuse me?" go into your spiel: "Listen, my husband [wife] is in the other room! I told you it was over and I meant it! It's over! We're through! And I'm not giving in to any more of your black-mail, either! You can keep the Porsche, but I'm not paying for the apartment or any more Beverly Hills shopping sprees, you got it? Now, get out of my life!" Hang up.

Originally published in *How to Get Rid of a Telemarketer* by Tony Dierckins and Tim Nyberg © 1996, Bad Dog Press

GO PLAY IN TRAFFIC!

Normally, an admonition to "go play in traffic" would be rather derogatory. But in this book, it's just another way to entertain yourself and others. While you've got to keep in mind that there's risk involved when playing with two thousand pounds of metal on wheels, it can also be a ton of fun. So be careful, and have fun!

Tire Crackers

Find some Bubble Wrap with one-inch bubbles at an office supply store or in a Dumpster behind a gift shop. Cut a strip about eighteen inches long and the width of a tire. Tape this to the tread of the front wheel(s) of a parked car. When the car starts moving, the resultant popping sounds like firecrackers.

Questionable Seating

If you're one of three guys in a pickup leaving a job site, make sure you sit on the far right side. When you see a girl, reach over and beep the horn and then duck down. The girl will look over to see two guys sitting smack up against each other.

Misbehavin' Car

If a friend is in the habit of leaving their car doors unlocked, sneak in and turn up the radio and turn on the windshield wipers, blinkers, and anything else that might confuse them. Sit back and watch as they turn on their car and confusion ensues!

Stinkin' Car Troubles

Hang twenty or more car-fresheners on the rearview mirror and drive with a gas mask on.

More Stinkin' Car Troubles

During the summer months, take some feta cheese, sardines, anchovies, or other odiferous foods, and place them behind the carpet on the firewall of your victim's car so the engine compartment heats them up enough to cause a big stink.

Getting "Punchy"

At work go around and collect all the little paper circles left in the paper punches. Then go to a friend or coworker's car and put them on top of the visor. Make sure to brush the strays off the seat. When your friend pulls the sun visor down, all the little circles will fall in their lap and face, simulating a snow shower. Alternatively, hide a fish (à la "More Stinkin' Car Troubles" above) on the driver's side visor. When the visor is lowered the fish will flop into the lap of the driver.

Frozen Window Dressing

In the winter when it's below 30°, cover your victim's car windows with wet paper towels or tissues.

My Windshield!

This is fun to play on someone who just had their windshield repaired. Cut a piece of plastic cling film in a large circle. Place it on your victim's windshield. Cut a baseball in half and place it on the top of the film. From a distance the cling film looks just like cracks coming out from the baseball.

About the Dent . . .

Write the following on a small piece of paper: "Sorry about the dent. You were parked awkwardly and I had some problems, but my insurance will cover it. Again, sorry." Scribble it quickly so it looks like you were in a hurry, but make it readable. Make up a name and phone number. Place it on one of those cars that has parked diagonally across two spaces so as to avoid door dings. Sit back and wait for the inspection and head scratching to take place.

Customize Your Vehicle

Mount a few propane tanks and various hoses, pipes, funnels and tubing to the top of your car. Write ALTERNATIVE PROPULSION RESEARCH VEHICLE—STAY BACK 200 FEET on your trunk.

Decorate your car like a parade float.

Get a large, fiberglass animal and mount it to the top of your car.

Mount taxidermied animals on various exterior car surfaces.

Weld ridiculously oversized fins on the rear quarter panels of your car.

Put opposing presidential candidates' bumper stickers on your rear bumper. Add derogatory stickers for each candidate.

Fill large clear food storage bags with water and gold fish and tape them to your side windows (driver and passenger snorkels and masks optional).

With vinyl letters from a sign shop, spell out STUPID DRIVER on the back of your car. At first glance it looks like STUDENT DRIVER—but then the truth of the matter is spelled out for all to see.

Mock Collision

Put a friend in the back of a pickup or van with a metal trash can and take a drive through a residential neighborhood at night. Come to a screeching halt while your friend slams the trash can down on the street. Then take off quickly. Count the porch lights coming on.

Horny Brakes

This one is great, but it takes a little mechanical know-how. Get two wires and alligator clips and rig up two jumpers. Go under your victim's hood and wire their horn to their brakes. This is a good prank to pull on the newlywed couples' getaway vehicle.

Fake Flat

Lay a three-foot strip of duct tape sticky side up on the roadway. When a car runs over it the tape will stick to the tire and flop around sounding like a flat tire.

Driving-Range Hazard

Pick the most obnoxiously expensive car in the country club parking lot and re-create the base-ball-in-the-windshield gag using half of a plastic golf ball.

Windshield Whizzers

Reaim your washer-fluid dispenser so when stopped at a traffic light you can squirt the car next to you.

Safe Driving Apparel

Wear a motorcycle helmet while driving. You may also want to don a gas mask to heighten the effect. Have a good story made up for when you get pulled over by the highway patrol. (The gas mask is for allergies and the helmet for extra protection in case the airbag accidentally inflates.)

Bird Droppings

You can create your own bird droppings with a can of whipped cream and a little shake of pepper. In the heat, the cream will run just like the real thing. Place the droppings strategically on door handles, in the middle of the windshield—any place that will cause your victim disgust and/or annoyance.

The Practical Joker's Handbook

Smoke-Covered Engine

Put a thin coating of motor oil or cooking oil on the engine of your victim's car. When the victim gets a couple of miles down the road and their car begins smoking profusely, they will assume the worst and be delayed for a time directly proportional to their wit or mechanical ability.

Manifold Breakfast

A few strips of bacon draped over the engine block will actually begin to cook as your victim is driving. They'll begin to wonder where the bacon smell is coming from. By the time they open their hood, the bacon should be nicely cooked. Or, the next time they get their oil changed, they'll have some explaining to do to their mechanic.

Beetles in Your Beetle

Those Japanese beetle traps don't kill the bugs; the bag just fills up with live beetles. Hundreds of 'em. Take the bag full of live beetles to a parking lot. The local video store is best, because people are in there for only a few minutes at a time. Look for a car where the windows are down only a few inches, and dump the beetles in there. Then wait for the owner of the car to come back.

Whoopy Exhaust

Cut off the flapping noise-making part and enough of the bladder of a whoopy cushion to fit over a car exhaust pipe. Duct tape it onto the pipe. When the car is running it will sound like cowboys relaxing around a campfire after a meal of Cookie's beans.

Engine Failure

Put a box in your engine compartment filled with
distributor caps, wires, fan belts, etc. Close the hood
and drive wherever there is a long line waiting on
the sidewalk. "Stall" the car in front of the line.
Get out mumbling about the "dang car!" Open the
hood, look inside, shrug your shoulders, scratch
your head, then proceed to pull stuff out of the
box and throw it on the road. Slam the hood, get
back into the car, start the engine, nod your head
to the crowd, smile, and drive off.

Bizarre Things to Do When Driving

Reminder: *Several of the following may result in serious injury or death (yourself and/or others). Or, worse yet, a moving violation—which will boost your auto insurance rates even higher. Use your head when deciding to actually implement any of these ideas. Many are fun to think about, but that's where their practicality ends. There. You have been warned.*

Drive in a chicken suit.

Pay the toll for the car behind you. Watch in the rearview mirror as the toll collector tries to explain to the next driver.

Laugh. Laugh a lot. Glance at neighboring cars, and laugh even more.

Put your arms down the legs of an extra pair of trousers, put sneakers on your hands, lean the seat back, and appear to drive with your "feet."

Drive backward through the bank drive-up teller line. This is especially effective if your passenger needs to make the transaction.

Honk frequently without motivation.

Vigorously wave at pedestrians and people in neighboring vehicles.

Disappearing Car

You're riding along with a friend who needs to stop at a store. When they go into the store, stay in the car and move it to a different parking spot. Watch as your friend tries to remember where he parked.

Disappearing Car Part II

Do the disappearing car gag, but this time park the car completely out of sight and lock the doors (remember to take the keys). Walk back to the parking space where you were left and stand waiting for your friend to return. Explain that you were carjacked.

The Practical Joker's Handbook

Auto Advantage

Tell your wife or girlfriend to stop off at the auto service station and "Have the air rotated in the tires. And Honey, while you're there, tell them to check the 'pressure relief valve' in the cab to make sure the windows don't pop out when it gets warm outside."

It's *Not* for *Sale!*

Take out an ad advertising a friend's brand-new vehicle for sale at thousands below its value. List the incredible "*Must Sell*" deal and your friend's phone number. Have the ad run one day only in the Saturday classifieds. Now, take your friend out to "paint the town red" until the wee hours of the morning. The next morning their phone will be ringing off the hook with offers for the vehicle.

Rooftop Soda

Attach a thirty-two-ounce soda cup to the top of your car with a large magnet inside the bottom of the cup, as if you had left it there by mistake. Drive merrily along with the radio *loud* so you can't hear the people yelling to you to get your drink off the car. When they point and wave, act like they are waving at you, smile, and wave back. You would not believe the reactions to this in traffic. People will *get out of their vehicles* and tap on the window to tell you about the cup! This also works well with an aluminum can and a double-sided wet suction cup.

Carcooning

Wrap your victim's car with cling wrap followed by a layer or two of duct tape. (The cling wrap is so you don't apply the tape directly to paint, which would have disastrous results.)

Ticket Madness

Get business-sized envelopes and draw a length-wise red stripe on the nonflap side of each envelope. Stick these envelopes under the wipers on a row of parked cars. At first glance it looks like all of the cars were ticketed.

Misplaced Horn

With your left thumb secretly activating the horn on the steering wheel, reach up to the dash or the car ceiling and push an imaginary horn button. Remark while beeping, "It's odd that they choose to put the horn button up here."

Cat's on the Roof

Have a passenger hold a handwritten sign up in the window that reads, IS THAT YOUR CAT ON TOP OF YOUR CAR? It's amazing how many people pull over and check.

Bees!

When pulled over for driving erratically, jump out of your car flailing your arms yelling, "*Bees!*" (This comes from the movie *Tommy Boy.*)

Directions, Please

Take an exit ramp from the highway and ask for directions to the town you're in. When they tell you you're already there, look confused, glance at your map, laugh, and exclaim, "Oh, wow! Wrong state!"

When Stopped at Intersections

Ask people in neighboring cars, "Pardon me. Do you have any Grey Poupon?" If they say no, offer them some. Small packets of Grey Poupon mustard are available at most deli counters.

Give puppet shows out of your side windows and/or sunroof. This is especially fun while waiting at intersections. It's even funnier if you seem to be totally oblivious to the puppet.

Eye the person in the next car suspiciously. With a look of fear, suddenly lock your doors.

Offer neighboring cars a nice selection of hors d'oeuvres.

Roll down your windows and blast talk radio. Head bang.

Get out of your car and place warning cones around you. Wait for the light to change, then quickly gather them up and drive off.

If your car has a quickly reclining driver's seat, pull up to stop at an intersection and quickly recline your seat. Neighboring cars will look over and see no driver.

Get out and squeegee your neighboring car's windshield.

Get a megaphone and sing along with the radio.

The Practical Joker's Handbook

WORK AND SCHOOL HUMOR BREAKS

WORK AND SCHOOL HUMOR BREAKS

You don't have to enjoy your job to have fun at work. These tried and true pranks can bring amusement to you and your coworkers in even the dullest of work situations. Since, I assume, some readers may still be in school and haven't yet entered the exciting world of full-time employment, I've included pranks and practical jokes you can pull in school. Please try to avoid expulsion.

Out of Order

Place an out of order sign on the executive wash-
room or opposite gender's restroom door.

Still in school? Place an out of order sign on
the staff/teacher's bathroom door.

Note: *For more bathroom pranks, see the Bathroom
Humor chapter (duh).*

Duct Taped Desk Drawer Dilemma

Duct tape is handy for driving your coworkers
nuts. Crawl under the desk and tape around the
underside edges of the center drawer. It won't
open—no matter how hard they pull. To add to
the confusion, leave the drawer slightly ajar before
taping it, so they can clearly see that it's not locked.

The Practical Joker's Handbook

Malfunctioning Mouse

Put a strip of clear tape over the mouse ball (opaque tape over optical sensors) on a computer mouse. Even when the mouse is moved, it still won't work.

Malfunctioning Mouse: The Sequel

If your computer sits back-to-back or adjacent to someone else's, unplug their mouse cord and replace it with yours. Their cursor will have a mind of its own.

Keyboard Confusion

To create a nonfunctioning keyboard, simply unplug the keyboard cable from the back of your victim's computer.

Monitor Mess

Dim the brightness control on everyone's monitors. Watch (and listen) as people frantically call tech support. (Make sure your monitor is dimmed also.)

Music (Forever) on Hold!

Remove the little music maker from a musical greeting card and hide it inside the earpiece of a coworker's telephone.

Thief!

If you work in a store with adhesive theft-control devices, slap one on the back of a fellow employee. They'll set off the alarm every time they walk through the front door.

Ash Blaster

If the lunch room/smoking room at work has plastic (or aluminum) ashtrays, make a small hole at the bottom and tape a small firecracker underneath with the wick coming up through the hole. Trim the wick and camouflage it with ashes and a few butts. When the victim sets his cigarette down ... *blam!* Ashes everywhere! And, you don't have to be around to get blamed, so you can do it again another time, when your coworkers have forgotten about it.

Call of the Wild

Leave the following message for someone who has left their desk for a few minutes: "A Mr. G. Raffe (or Mr. L. E. Phont) called and would like you to call them back." Leave the number for the local zoo.

Booby-Trapped Snack

Start with a can of fruit cocktail or any kind of fruit. With a can opener, remove the entire bottom of the can and empty the contents. Turn it upside down and fill it with steel ball bearings. (Marbles will also do.) Put a piece of cardboard under it and turn it over onto a coworkers desk. Make sure you place it close to the edge. Leave a napkin, spoon, and a note telling them to enjoy the little snack you left for them.

Spit Take

In a band? Tape the spit valve open on a trumpet and watch the guy try to figure out what's wrong with the horn.

"Hello Steve. This is Hal."

If you work in an office where two computer workstations are set up back to back, you can pull this one off. Before the person who works across from you gets to his station, unplug his keyboard and plug yours into his computer. Then open a word processor document on his terminal. When he sits down start typing something like this:

"Hello, [your victim's name]. How are you doing today? My name is Hal, [your victim's name]. I'd appreciate it if you wouldn't pound on my keys so hard when you type. . . ."

Dialing for XXX

In case you missed this in the Phone Phunnies Chapter: Change your boss's speed-dial numbers to massage parlor and escort service numbers.

Quickie Office Pranks and Gags

Here is a list of miscellaneous silliness you can use to relieve workplace boredom.

Caution: These may cause people to question your sanity and possibly lead to a standing position in the unemployment line. Until that time, have fun!

Page yourself over the intercom. Don't disguise your voice.

Every time someone asks you to do something, ask, "Do you want fries with that?"

Encourage your colleagues to join you in synchronized rolling desk chair dancing.

Put your garbage can on your desk and label it "IN."

Develop an unnatural fear of staplers.

Put decaf in the coffee maker for three weeks. Once everyone has gotten over their caffeine addictions, switch back to caffeinated.

Reply to everything someone says with, "That's what you think."

Finish all your sentences with "In accordance with the prophecy."

dont use any punctuation or capital letters in your reports

As often as possible, skip rather than walk.

Send e-mail to the rest of the company to tell them what you're doing. For example, "If anyone needs me, I'll be in the bathroom in Stall #3."

Put mosquito netting around your cubicle. Play a tape of jungle sounds all day.

Do puppet shows over the top edge of your cubical.

Show up for work in a rented mascot costume.

On casual Friday show up for work in formal attire.

Tell your boss, "It's not the voices in my head that bother me, it's the voices in your head."

During a meeting, swat at flies that don't exist.

If Your Business Has an Elevator

When there's only one other person in the elevator, tap them on the shoulder, then pretend it wasn't you.

Ask if you can push floor buttons for anyone— then push the wrong buttons.

Call the psychic hotline from the elevator phone and ask them if they know what floor you are on.

Move your desk and chair into the elevator. When the door opens to let someone on, ask if they have an appointment.

Lay a Twister mat on the elevator floor and ask occupants if they want to play.

Ask, "Whoa! Did you feel that?!"

In a crowded elevator ask a coworker, "Are you still contagious?"

When the doors close, announce to the other occupants, "It's okay, don't panic, they open again."

When riding the elevator alone, face the back wall. The door will open and riders will seldom get on the elevator with you.

Talk to other occupants only through the use of a hand puppet.

Listen to the elevator walls with a stethoscope.

Sweater Binder

If you have a coworker who leaves their sweater on their chair as the temperature in the office fluctuates, this one is for you! When they're not around, use small binder clips to bind the inside of the sleeve shut. Better yet, if you're quick with a needle and thread, put a couple of loose stitches through the sweater cuffs or sew the cuffs to the hem of the sweater.

Staple Slammer

If you have a coworker who is continually banging their stapler, get a little snap firecracker (the kind you throw down on the sidewalk). Place the snap into the staple chamber. The next time they hit the stapler, it will hit back.

Staple Diet

Secretly empty a coworker's stapler. Then (before they've had time to refill the stapler) visit their desk with a Post-it note in your hand and then proceed to "staple" it to your forehead with their stapler. This is believable because you have the element of surprise going for you, and because prior to your visit, you have prepared the Post-it by drawing a small black line on the side opposite the sticky stripe which, at first glance, appears to be a staple.

Malfunctioning Marker

If you have a teacher or coworker who loves writing on an erasable white board during meetings, mess them up by supergluing the caps on all of the markers.

This Is a Test

Teachers: This is one prank that will get your students and teach them a valuable lesson at the same time. When passing out a test give the following directions: "Read through all of the questions first. You will have fifty-five minutes to complete the test." Of course, they probably won't listen, and won't read through all of the questions first. The last question should read: "Do not complete any of the questions on this test. Turn in a blank test paper with your name on it and you will get an 'A.'"

Peanut-Packed

If your office cubicle walls are tall enough that you can't see over the walls, duct tape plastic wrap to both sides of the doorway and fill the doorway cavity with Styrofoam packing peanuts. It will give the appearance of the entire cubicle being filled.

Heavy Load

Get a large empty carton (computer monitor cartons work well) and seal it with packaging tape. Carry it into a colleague's workspace with great difficulty, as if it's extremely heavy. Set it carefully on their floor and say, "This came for you." When they muster up the strength to move it, they'll most likely fall right on their butt.

Walking on Nails

The clear plastic carpet protectors that enable office chairs to roll easily on thick carpet often have *very* sharp points on the bottom to hold them in place. If you have someone in your office who tends to work in stocking feet, flip their chair mat over when they leave their desk for a moment. They will experience a surprisingly painful return.

The Funnel Trick

In your workplace, grab several friends and fill your morning coffee cups with water. Stand around while one guy sticks a funnel in the top of his pants and holds a quarter. When the unsuspecting victim walks in, the funnel guy should start rolling the quarter down and off the end of his nose, purposely missing the funnel. When the victim asks what's happening, tell him you're trying to catch the quarter in the funnel. Invariably he will say, "That's easy," or "That shouldn't be hard to do." Respond with, "Oh yeah? Bet you can't get it in six tries." As soon as he sticks the funnel in his pants and tilts back his head, have everybody reach out and dump their cup of water down the funnel.

The Practical Joker's Handbook

Smear Tactics

Dip the end of your middle finger into something wet, then slip your wet finger into a used ashtray. Ashes will stick to your finger. Tell your victim that they have something on their cheek. Point with your index finger, tucking your middle finger into your palm. After they wipe their face say, "No, sorry you missed it! Here, let me get it!" When you reach up, rub the ashes onto their face two or three times, leaving behind a *big* black stripe or *large* smudge on their cheek. Since they cannot see their own face till they get to a mirror, they will walk around without knowing the smudge is there.

Note: This is a good one to pull on someone just before they walk into a company meeting.

Carpenter Capers

It's always fun to play jokes on rookie carpenters. Many newcomers have a fear of power tools in general, and saws in particular. To take advantage of this, assign your victim the task of sawing a hole in a wall with a saber saw. Instruct them to be *sure* nobody is behind the wall before they start cutting. When they start sawing, sneak behind the wall with a piece of wood and a squirt bottle of ketchup. Push the wood into the saw blade while squirting the ketchup on the blade and screaming.

A Date for the Boss

Prior to your next office party, photocopy a picture of your boss and add their real phone number, advertising "Need a date to the Christmas Party. Please call . . ." Plaster the posters in strategic locations around the office or around town.

Sinking Chairs

Most office dwellers have chairs that use a pneumatic piston to control the height. The person's weight is used to cause the downward adjustment. While your coworker is away from their desk, use a strip of duct tape to tape the height-adjusting lever to the bottom of the seat. When they sit down, their weight will cause the chair to bottom out quickly.

(See the Drive-Thru Humor chapter for fast-food worker ideas.)

More Workplace Wackiness

Put a chair facing a printer. Sit there all day and tell people you're waiting for your document.

Every time someone asks you to do something, ask them to sign a waiver.

Name all your pens and insist that meetings can't begin until they're all present.

Come to work in your pajamas.

Put a picture of your mother on your business card.

Make up nicknames for all your coworkers and refer to them only by these names. "That's a good point, Sparky." "No, I'm sorry. I'm going to have to disagree with you there, Sport."

Include a piece of your children's artwork as a cover page for all reports that you write. (If you don't have children, draw stick figures yourself.)

Schedule meetings for 4:14 p.m. When everyone gets to the meeting, tell them to go home.

Volunteer to organize the company Christmas party. Hold it at a McDonald's Playland. Charge everyone $15 each.

No matter what anyone asks you, reply "Okay" while nodding.

Have two identical coffee mugs. Grow mold in one and leave it on your desk when your real mug is not in use.

Put on your headphones whenever the boss comes into the office. Talk in a loud voice. Remove your headphones when he or she leaves.

When in conversation, no matter where you are in the office, mutter, "I think my phone is ringing" and leave. Go get a coffee.

Install a set of buttons and lights in the arm of your chair.

Replace your boss's photo of his wife with a photo of a Victoria's Secret model.

Talk into your pen or pocket calendar.

Tape Christmas lights around the top of your cubicle.

Put a plastic pink flamingo at each side of your cubical entrance.

Bring in meals that didn't turn out quite right as special treats for your coworkers.

Decorate your office with pictures of child television stars. Insist that they are your children.

For a relaxing break, get away from it all with a mask and snorkel in the company fish tank.

When you go to a party at a coworker's house, don't automatically assume that the drinks are free. Ask, and ask often.

Fun with E-mail

Determine how many cups of coffee are "too many" and send a memo about it to your coworkers.

Send blind e-mail messages announcing "Free pizza and doughnuts in the lunchroom!" When people complain that there was none, just lean back, pat your stomach, and say, "Oh, you've got to be faster than that." Do this continually until nobody believes you anymore. Then order in pizzas and doughnuts in the lunchroom.

Include a personal note on every e-mail you send. "On a personal note, I'm feeling a bit tired and grumpy today." Or, "On a personal note, I'm pleased to announce that I got my highest score ever on Tetris last night."

Compose all your e-mail in rhyming couplets.

Subscribe your bosses' e-mail address to questionable Internet services.

Send e-mail to yourself engaging yourself in an intelligent debate about the direction of one of your company's products. Forward the mail to a coworker and ask them to settle the disagreement.

Send your coworkers an e-mail stating that the FBI Sexual Predator Task Force has seized your computer for certain questionable images they discovered on your hard drive. State that your attorney has informed you that the FBI is tracking down everyone you've exchanged e-mails with for the past two years and is issuing warrants to check the contents of their computers.

FUN ON
THE TOWN

FUN ON THE TOWN

The world is full of crazy people—why not join in? It's always fun to make people wonder what you're up to—especially complete strangers. Here are some suggestions for having fun around town.

Authorized Personnel Only!

Go to a store and post a big sign on the front door that reads AUTHORIZED PERSONNEL ONLY.

Congratulation is in (Dis)Order

Spray paint large signs and attach to the front of your victim's house. For instance:

CONGRATS SMITHS, STATE SQUARE-DANCING CHAMPIONS!

CONGRATS, SMITHS, ON YOUR PREGNANCY!

CONGRATS SMITHS, PUBLISHER'S CLEARING HOUSE RUNNERS-UP!

ATM Jackpot!

When the money comes out of the ATM, scream, "I won! I won! That's the third time this week!"

The Practical Joker's Handbook

Frame-a-Friend

Sometimes when you buy used videos from
Blockbuster, they still have the little theft strip on
them. Carefully remove the theft strip and duct
tape it to the bottom of a friend's shoe. Send the
friend on a run to the video store.

A Generous Gift Indeed

Get a gift card at a local department store and spend
all but a small amount (fifty-eight cents or so). Place
the gift card in a greeting card and give it to a friend.

Animals on the Loose!

When leaving the zoo, start running toward
the parking lot, yelling, "Run for your lives!
They're loose!"

You Won the Lottery!

If you have a local lottery where you get to pick your own numbers, buy a fresh newspaper with last night's winning numbers then buy those very same numbers. With great excitement show off your winning numbers to your family and friends.

A Lousy Trick!

This one is for people with long hair. Next time you are standing in line with a lot of people, have a Tic Tac hidden in your hand and start to pick in your hair. After a few minutes of digging, act like you just pulled a huge louse out of your hair, and eat it! People will squirm.

Seventeen Cigarettes

Take a soft pack of cigarettes out of your victim's carton. Carefully cut the bottom cellophane and open the pack from the bottom. Remove three or more cigarettes (but less than five as this will become noticeable) and glue the pack back up with clear-drying glue. Stand back and watch as your victim realizes they have purchased a "new" pack with less than twenty cigarettes.

Stuck-Up Butts

Carefully slit open the bottom flap of a new pack of cigarettes. Apply glue to the entire inside bottom of the flap, and then reseal it. When your victim opens the "new" pack from their carton, they can shake as hard as they like, but the butts won't come out.

Lunchtime Speed Trap

At lunch time, eat in your car and have some fun at the same time. Park your car just off a main road. Roll down your window and point a hair dryer at passing cars. See if they slow down.

Giant Underpants

Buy a pair of giant underpants and go to the laundromat. Find the smallest person there and wait until they look away. Slip the underpants into their dryer and wait for the hilarity to ensue. First you get to see them hold the underpants up as they try to fold them, then you get to watch them ask people if the underwear is theirs.

The Practical Joker's Handbook

Secret Surfin'

Purchase a universal remote, enter the appropriate television code, and secretly change channels at your favorite sports bar.

Basement Sale

Place an ad in the paper for a basement sale at a friend's house. (Of course, they won't be aware that they are going to have a sale). Advertise antiques, baby clothes, guns, etc., and that the sale is Saturday—door opens at 7 a.m. Very early on the morning of the day of the "sale," put up a sign on your victim's front door: BASEMENT SALE: PLEASE USE BACK DOOR. Keeping the victim out late the night before will add to their confused stupor the next day as eager sale goers rap at their back door.

Money-Saving Sale

You can pull off the same prank without the cost of the newspaper ad—just make road signs advertising the sale: ESTATE SALE—EVERYTHING MUST GO!

Again, make sure you advertise an early start hour or the signs will be removed before anyone visits the sale.

For Sale by Owner

When your victim is out of town, stick a HOME FOR SALE sign in their front yard with their cell phone number on it. Somewhere on the sign also write EMERGENCY RELOCATION—MUST SELL BY END OF WEEK—PLEASE MAKE OFFER.

The Practical Joker's Handbook

Open House

"Borrow" some real estate open house signs (return them when you are done), and place them in front of your friend's house about 8:00 on a Sunday morning. If they sleep in on Sunday, they will be awakened by someone wanting to look at their house.

Vote for Someone Else

In the height of election season, drive around town at night and switch around all of the lawn signs.

Little Squirt on the Beach

Take water guns to the beach and act like you are sleeping in your lounge chair. As people walk by, discreetly squirt them but keep your eyes barely open.

Malfunction Junction

When you are the first person to a crosswalk, pretend to push the button, but don't actually push it. Act agitated and complain about the city's electrical wiring. Fake push the button a couple more times. Then, fume as you wait for the walk light to appear. Seventy-five percent of the time, the other people never think to hit the button themselves!

Walk Light Button Short

Get a sparking ring (sometimes called "funkin' ring") at a local magic or prank store. Walk up to a crosswalk and push the walk light button while triggering the spark ring. A shower of sparks will appear to emit from the button. Let out a loud "*ouch!*" and shake off the "pain" of the shock. Tell someone else to try the button. This trick works in elevators, too.

Taste Test

Apply a nasty substance (like car grease or anything else you wouldn't want to put in your mouth) to your index finger. As you lift your hand to your mouth, switch to your middle finger and place it in your mouth. Remark on the taste.

The Maddening Marshmallow Man

Buy a bag of jumbo-sized marshmallows from a grocery store and then head to the nearest golf course. Stand in the rough along the fairway and wait for someone teeing off to yell "fore!" When their ball is lofting toward your vicinity, throw the marshmallows all over the fairway. It's nearly impossible to locate their ball(s) from a distance with marshmallows all over the grass!

Abdominal Alien Birth

This looks really weird! When you are wearing a loose, oversized sweatshirt or sweater, pull one of your arms out of the sleeve and tuck it next to your stomach.

With your exposed hand, grab the cuff of the empty sweater arm. Extend both sleeves straight down toward your crotch. Now is when the fun begins. Walk into a crowd and start alternately raising and lowering your "arms" and your hidden arm (from the middle of your stomach). It appears as if you are holding your hands, swinging your arms up to chest level, and back down while an alien is popping in and out of your stomach.

Third Arm

Here's another one you can do while wearing a large sweatshirt or sweater: Prepare by tucking your empty sleeve into your front pants pocket. Get into a conversation in which you gesture with your exposed arm while talking. Without warning or recognition on your part, make a "third" hand come out of your neckline and scratch your chin.

Cheeky Humor

When in a conversation with someone, keep glancing at a certain spot on their cheek. Regain eye contact only long enough to make it obvious that your eyes once again move to the same spot on their cheek. Eventually they will give their cheek a little flick with their hand. If they need a little encouragement, brush your own cheek while staring at theirs.

Official Notice

Picking up mail for a vacationing neighbor? If you get a general notice in the mail from the town or village of your residence, chances are your neighbor will be getting one too. Open yours to see what it is. If not important, make a photocopy of the letterhead with the body of the letter covered with white paper. On this new "official letterhead," you can compose any notice that you want. Replace their notice with the fake, and sit back and wait for them to read their mail. I used this prank to write a letter proposing a bowling alley/nightclub in our residential neighborhood and inviting neighbors to the next council meeting if they wanted to voice objection. The recipient of the letter showed up at the meeting as mad as a hornet!

Public Sneezer #1

Walk down the street and fake sneeze on people you pass. A friend following close behind you can provide the spray with a bottle of water.

Public Sneezer #2

After getting a drink at a public fountain, get your hand wet. Fake-sneeze on a friend. The spray is provided by a flick of your hand while going up to "cover your sneeze."

Grocery Planting

Depending on your disposition, you can play this joke on friends or total strangers. While grocery shopping, people often leave their cart unattended while grabbing an item off of the shelf. Take this opportunity to slip unwanted items into their cart. They generally won't discover the mystery items until they reach the checkout, sometimes not until they reach home. The more bizarre the items you introduce into their cart, the funnier the outcome. Consider canned fish balls (yes, they do exist), cans of Spam, ugly fruit, head cheese, pickled pigs feet, etc.

Grocery Stalking

If you ever catch a friend, relative, or neighbor arriving home from the grocery store with a trunk load of groceries, wait until they go into the house with their first bags. Then, quickly remove two more bags of groceries from their car and duck out of sight. Keep removing and replacing groceries (with and without the bags) until you get caught. They will generally become so bewildered that they will be relieved to find out that it was only you "assisting" them.

Drive-by Breading

A new twist on TP'ing someone's home: Get a bunch of bread from a Dumpster behind a local bakery or bakery discount shop. Wait until dark, unwrap the bread, and dump it all over a victim's lawn. The more bread you have, the more surprising and peculiar the prank will be.

Fiery Poop Sack

Note: *This is an old joke that has been practiced for years at Halloween time. It's so cruel and messy that I've awarded it a sad face (not recommended). Nevertheless, it is a classic and therefore probably warrants publishing.*

Fill a paper bag with dog poop. Place the paper bag on somebody's front porch and then light the bag on fire. Quickly ring the doorbell and run, making sure you can't be seen. When the victim opens the door, they'll freak out at the fire and try to stomp it out. As they are extinguishing the messy bag at the front door, run around the house to the back door and knock there, too. Guess what happens to the carpet when the victim runs through the house to catch the prankster at the backdoor!

Movie Madness

This is best if done by a large group. Each person should attempt to enter a movie theater carrying a folding chair under their arm. When asked, say that you prefer this to the theater chairs. Or, volunteer that you are a group of people working through their phobias. "This week we are working on our public seating phobia. By the end of the movie, our goal is for all of us to be sitting in your seats."

3-D Movie Madness

Enter a movie theater (or an airplane that will be featuring an in-flight movie) wearing 3-D glasses. Assure the attendant and the other moviegoers that they'll work at *any* movie.

Look, Up in the Sky!

Stand in the middle of an open air mall (or any other crowded area) with a friend. Start looking up at the sky, pointing, and talking quietly to each other about what you "see." In a bit you should have a crowd gathered—all looking up, at which time you quietly leave the area.

The Omnipresent Clergy

Secretly turn on your preacher's cordless microphone while he's greeting people, going to the bathroom, etc.

Hold That Tiger

For this one you need a rope and a friend. Hold
one end of the rope while your friend holds the
other. Tighten the rope around a corner on a
building. Ask a stranger on the street if he would
care to help you hold the rope for a few minutes,
while you are off to collect something. Tell them,
"If you have to leave, please find someone else to
hold the rope until you return." Then, walk away.
Have your friend on the other end of the rope
do the same. The result: two complete strangers
around a corner holding a rope wondering why
they're holding a rope.

You'll Have to Speak Up

Tell two strangers who are about to meet for the first time that the other is very hard of hearing. Tell them both that the other is very sensitive about it, so talk loudly, but try not to be obvious about it. Whatever they do, they shouldn't mention it. (It's also fun to tell all your coworkers the same about a new employee and watch everyone shout at him all day.)

Monkey Business

Run into a party (or any gathering of people) out of breath and wheezing. Between breaths ask if they'd heard about all the monkeys on Main Street (or another well-known local street). Everyone will ask what you're jabbering about. Tell them a "monkey truck" tipped over on Main Street and monkeys are everywhere! Usually a group will run to the "crash site" to see the monkeys.

The Practical Joker's Handbook

Spontaneous Combustion in the Tanning Parlor

Take an extra set of clothes and leave them on the chair. Then pour a little pile of ashes in the closed tanning bed.

More Tanning-Parlor Terror

Get some really gross pictures of people with skin cancers. Plaster the wall in the tanning room with them. Distribute brochures telling of the horrors of ultraviolet radiation all over the waiting area. Plant some more in the waiting room magazines.

Still More Tanning-Parlor Terror

Go out at night and catch a whole bunch of moths. Release them in the salon. When a tanning bed is lit up, they will be attracted to it and buzz the occupant.

A Noisy Joke

Sneak up to someone's house in the middle of the night and duct tape their doorbell down. This works if they have a bell that keeps making noise when the button is depressed.

Noisier Joke

This one will cost you a few bucks, but it's probably worth it. Tape the trigger on an air horn and toss it onto your victim's roof. It'll blow until the can runs out of compressed air.

Department Store Daffiness

Today's massive megastores can be cold, impersonal, and, admit it, disheartening. But, they can also provide a venue for fun. But remember, Big Brother is usually watching your every move. So have an excuse ready when you are approached by security.

Set all of the alarm clocks to go off at ten-minute increments throughout the day.

Ride a display bicycle through the aisles. If stopped, tell them you are taking it for a test-drive.

Walk up to total strangers and say, "I haven't seen you for so long! How have you been?" See if they act as if they know who you are.

Retune all of the radios to an opera or polka station.

When you sense people behind you in the aisle, walk very slowly, as if oblivious to their presence. Weave slightly so they can't pass.

Start up a game of Marco Polo with your friends in various parts of the store.

When an announcement comes over the loudspeaker, duck down in a fetal position with your hands over your ears and scream, "No! It's those voices again!"

If you ever notice an employee using a phone to make a public address page, watch the access number they dial. Find a secluded phone, dial up, and make your own announcements.

Dart around the aisles in a stealthlike position singing the *Mission Impossible* theme song.

Fall asleep in the patio furniture.

If there is a tent set up in sporting goods, crawl inside. Poke your head out to tell passersby that they can join you if they go over to bedding and get a couple of pillows.

Get down on your hands and knees and test-drive toy cars and trucks. (Best if you are over forty.)

Relocate unattended shopping carts. Watch as shoppers try to figure out where they left their cart.

Pull a folding chair into the magazine aisle and make yourself at home with a magazine and a cold beverage from the snack counter.

Attempt to put a bag of candy on layaway.

DINING
OUTRAGEOUSLY

DINING OUTRAGEOUSLY

Sure, it's fun to eat out. But it can be even more fun if you use some of these strange little activities to spice up your meal.

Note: *Restaurant joking etiquette: If you play a joke that leaves a mess, be nice and help clean it up. If the joke is at the expense of the server, tip well!*

Saltshaker Shenanigans

You did it as a kid, why not keep up the mischief when you're older? Unscrew the saltshaker top and replace it very loosely. The next person who uses it will be on a high-sodium diet.

Confused Gender Shakers

Unscrew the top of a saltshaker. Place a napkin "gasket" over the top of the shaker and, before you screw the top back on, fill the cap with pepper. Replace the lid and tear off the excess napkin. The next person to use the salt will deliver a pile of pepper onto their food. You can rig the pepper shaker the same way with salt.

The Practical Joker's Handbook

Saltshaker Volcano

A bit of a twist on the old loosening-the-saltshaker gag. Get an opaque salt shaker and put a small amount of vinegar in it. Fill the lid with baking soda and make a napkin gasket between the lid and the body of the shaker. When a person tries to use the salt, the vinegar will react with the baking soda causing a grade-school volcano effect.

Tic Tac Teeth

When you see your server coming your way, slip a few white Tic Tacs in your mouth. When the server asks how everything is, stick your tongue in your cheek and with labored speech say, "I didn't want to complain, but the steak is a little tough . . ." Then, spit out the Tic Tacs as if you've lost a few teeth trying to chew the meat.

It Prevents Me from "Streaking"

Going to a restaurant can be boring sometimes, but it can be spiced up if you produce a Windex or other glass cleaner plastic spray bottle and spray your food, saying, "It just doesn't have the zing that I like." Then, unscrew the top and take a couple of swigs and put it away. Make darned sure you've cleaned the original contents out of the bottle well, first, because it's poisonous. Use two or three drops of blue food coloring in water (or a blue sports drink) to get just the right color.

Note: In his act, comedian The Amazing Jonathan takes a swig out of a Windex bottle and comments, "It keeps me from streaking."

Seat Protectors

When being seated at a restaurant, without comment (and in plain view of the host), have each person in your party pull out a toilet seat protector (the kind you find in restrooms) and place it on their chair prior to sitting.

Menu Madness

When at a restaurant, tell the server your order while pointing at a different item on the menu. Do this for every item from appetizers to dessert, including beverages. When they attempt to clarify your request say, "No, the [request the same item]." This time point to yet another item. Remember to tip well.

Heartthrob Beef

This one is hilarious and has even gotten me a few free meals. Get a "plate lifter" at your local joke/novelty shop. This is a long tube with a little bladder on one end and a bulb on the other. The original joke was to hide the bladder under the tablecloth to make plates jump up and down when the bulb was squeezed. But I found a better use.

Order a burger or steak to your liking. When the plate is delivered and the server has left, rig the steak or burger with the bladder under the meat and run the tube off the side of the plate (hidden by garnish) to the bulb, which you can operate with your hand under the table. When the server walks by, call their attention to the meat which must be undercooked, as it still has a heart-beat! (The plate lifter is causing the meat to throb in a heartbeat-like rhythm.) The server usually gets bug-eyed and says, I'm sorry, I'll have them cook it longer. Before they take the plate, tell them to

leave the plate and bring the manager over. Once a crowd is drawn and all are sufficiently horrified, reveal the secret. I've had brighter managers catch on right away but tell me that they "want to bring the chef out to see that!"

Birthday Bluster

My favorite joke has got to be the old "it's your birthday!" prank. Take a friend to a restaurant that you *know* makes a fuss when its someone's birthday. When your dining guest is in the restroom or at the salad bar, notify the staff that it is their birthday and that they will probably deny it. But ignore what they say; they *never* want people to make a big deal about their birthday. Watch hilarity ensue as they are fussed over and try to deny that it is their birthday.

Dr. (Hot) Pepper

Wait for your victim to set their drink down. Rub tabasco sauce or a habanero pepper on the rim of their can or glass. Watch as they take a drink and about two or three seconds later realize that their mouth is growing hotter and hotter. (*Caution*: Don't rub your eyes or you will become the burn victim! Also, be aware that some people may have allergies to peppers.) Be ready to purchase the victim a new drink.

Dribble Can

While someone isn't looking, place a small pinhole in the side of their soda/pop/beer can just below where they drink. Every time they drink they will dribble on themselves.

Little Suckers

Little Sucker One: When a friend is drinking out of a paper cup with a straw and lid, wait until they leave their drink unattended and tie a knot in their straw below the lid.

Little Sucker Two: Same setup. This time, put a little pinhole in the straw just below the lid.

Little Sucker Three: Same setup. This time, snip the straw about a half inch below the lid.

Little Sucker Four: Same setup, but replace their straw with a new straw that you've rigged with a load of baking soda or flour.

JA-LOP-IN-OHS

Purposely pronounce menu items wrong. For instance jalapeños (*hal i PEEN yos*) becomes *Ja LOP in ohs*.

Name Your Own Buffet

Here's a good one for those Chinese all-you-can-eat buffets: Usually, the buffets have little signs above the sneeze guard telling what the buffet item is. Note the size and color of the signs and bring your own replacement signs next time you visit the buffet. Here are some suggestions: Dog Mein, Chicken PooPoo, Fried Lice, Plate Scrapings with Oyster Sauce, Beef with Pea Frogs, Mooey Gooey Guy Broth . . . you get the idea.

Create Your Own Special

Those little plastic table tent holders usually have removable special cards. Often times these cards are blank on the back. This is your opportunity to make up your own special. My favorite is PRUNE PIE: TO GO! $2.95.

Chicken Fingers

Next time you order chicken fingers (usually breaded breast fillets) tell your server, "I'd really like to try those chicken fingers." Then overreact when they're delivered to the table: "*Man!* That was some *huge* chicken! I mean think of it! These fingers are bigger than mine! That sucker must have been four hundred pounds easy! Must have been a Texas chicken. . . . Personally, I was surprised to find out that chickens even *had* fingers!" (Continue for an uncomfortably long time.)

Peppered Ice Cream

When delivered a dish of ice cream, nonchalantly begin peppering it. When someone comments, insist that it really brings out the flavor. (Actually, you can't really taste the pepper.)

Sorry, We're Out of That

If you overhear your server tell another table that the restaurant is out of an item (let's say cheesy fries), order a whole list of food, including the cheesy fries. Your server will apologize and inform you that they are out of cheesy fries. At which time you decrease your list by one item—still including the cheesy fries. The dialogue will continue:

"No, I'm sorry, we're all out of cheesy fries."

"Oh, well, then just get me [all items again, minus one] and cheesy fries."

Repeat until you are down to just the cheesy fries.

"Well then, just give me an order of cheesy fries."

DRIVE-THRU HUMOR

DRIVE-THRU HUMOR

Messin' around with minimum-wage-earning fast-food employees may be fun for you and the people in your car, but, depending on what kind of day the employee has been having, you run the risk of ending up with foreign items in your food (and I don't mean Brazilian beef).

Guide Me In

Have one of your passengers get out of the car and direct you through the fast-food drive-up window as if parking an airplane at a gate. A flashlight in each hand heightens the effect at night.

To Go

When going through the fast-food drive-thru, specify that the order is "to go." Repeat this several times throughout the order.

Disgruntled Drive-Thru Patron

If you're on the drive-thru side of the speaker, turn it around. When they ask, "Would you like fries with that?" Repeat their question, then say nothing. "Would I like fries with that?" Repeat as long as possible.

Broken Speaker

Go to a fast-food drive-thru with a speaker system and post a big sign in red letters on the speaker that reads SPEAKER IS BROKEN. PLEASE SPEAK LOUDLY AND SLOWLY. Park your car within earshot of the speaker, then watch and listen for the shouting to begin.

McJoking

At the McDonald's drive-thru, order everything with the word Mc in front of it. McCoke, McFries, McQuarter Pounder with McCheese . . . and, it never hurts to throw in a Mick Jagger for good measure.

What Else Can You Spell?

Next time you go through the drive-thru with
a friend, tell them you heard they had a new
promotion. If you go through the drive-thru saying,
"I can spell Super Combo," they will give you a
free hamburger.

Speaker Problems

Pull into a fast-food drive-thru and give your entire
order talking through a kazoo. It replicates the bad
speaker sound that you are forced to endure.

Wrong Restaurant, Dude

Order items only sold at a competing fast-food
restaurant. When they correct you, select items
from another fast-food restaurant's menu.

If you are a fast-food worker . . .

Fast Food Dribble Cups

This testimonial from a fast-food worker: "While working in a fast-food establishment, I found rude drive-thru customers to be a pain in the keester. To 'enrich' the lives of my rude customers I'd stick a small hole in the bottom of their beverage. Since the pinhole wasn't large, the customer usually didn't notice it until the cup sat in their lap for several minutes and they had a wet crotch."

To Go?

If you work at a fast-food drive-thru window, ask your customers, "Would you like that to go?"

Disgruntled Fast-Food Worker

When the boss isn't looking (or listening), try this: Repeat everything the customer orders in the form of a question. For instance: "I'll have a quarter pounder with cheese and fries." Answer, "Would you like fries with that? Would you like to upsize that to a full quarter pounder? Would you like to add cheese to your quarter pounder?" Space out the questions so they have time to repeat their order between each inane round of questioning.

The Practical Joker's Handbook

EPILOGUE

Well, that should keep you busy for a while. Remember the "rules" for practical joking that I listed in the introduction. If you come up with any variations or new ideas that you'd like to share, submit them to my Web site: www.practicaljokebook.com.

Have fun! And watch your back!

NOTES

NOTES

NOTES

NOTES